A WOMAN BUSINESS BUILDER: 5 SIGNIFICANT ABILITIES A STARTUP LADY ENTREPRENUERER MUST POSSESS

MADISON E. BONHAM

Table of Content

INTRODUCTION

CHAPTER 1

Meaning of "Lady Entrepreneur"

Highlights of Ladies Business Endeavor

Why Do Women Enter the Corporate World?

Factors Affecting a Lady Entrepreneur

CHAPTER 2

Business Advice for Women With an Entrepreneurial Spirit

Women Entrepreneurs' Obstacles to Starting a Business and How to Overcome Them

CHAPTER 3

The Executives Way a Woman Entrepreneur may Build others as a Side Project to her Business

The Best Approach to Handling your Family and Business

CHAPTER 4

Qualities a Woman Entrepreneur Should Possess:

Critical Areas to Focus on to Grow Your Business as a Woman Entrepreneur

CHAPTER 5

The Best Way For a Female Entrepreneur, to Adjust Business and Daily Life.

CONCLUSION

INTRODUCTION

The study of women entrepreneurs has grown significantly in recent years, earning widespread acceptance among academics and making a significant contribution, above all, to understanding all the variables that explain why it is challenging for women to pursue an entrepreneur career. Many scholars have been interested in female entrepreneurs recently, who are the group of business people with the fastest global growth.

Due to the fact that it creates job possibilities and encourages independence, women's entrepreneurship is essential for both the improvement of society and the country's economy. In order to battle poverty, hunger, and sickness and to promote economic growth, gender equality and the empowerment of women are essential.

Sustainable economic growth Although it is widely acknowledged that a nation's ability to compete depends on the active participation of women in industry, politics, and education, as well as current gender stereotypes that are strongly embedded in a country's sociocultural background, study, and development. can be a difficult limitation. In fact, gender and culture interact constantly, influencing gender roles and identities as well as the economic and social context in which women's entrepreneurship is rooted.

Madison.

CHAPTER 1

Meaning of "Lady Entrepreneur"

The women or a group of women who initiate, plan, and carry out a business venture might be referred to as women Lady Entrepreneur. To be referred to be Lady entrepreneurs, women must advance, model, or engage in a financial activity. Entrepreneurial women with a vision are the ones that look into innovative approaches to financial inclusion and commitment. In Canada, England, Germany, Australia, and the US, female business visionaries have had a significant impact on every sector of the economy. The industries chosen by women include retail trade, restaurants, hotels, education, social services, housekeeping, security, and manufacturing. For the following reasons, they have impacted business:

(I) They need fresh challenges that provide opportunities for self-fulfillment.

(ii) They must show their guts in competitive and inventive situations.

(iii) They feel that the adjustment should regulate the balance between their work and family commitments. Montreal observes Dina Lavoie, a teacher of business venture, "Women business owners often hire a small number of employees, while males are required to have nine or more employees. A small company often matches a woman's lifestyle. The extension might indicate a lack of control or disruption in how much time and energy she devotes to various aspects of her life. She could also need to plan out and organize every aspect of her life. She could fear that if she grows to a point where she can't manage and control every aspect of her firm, she will lose that opportunity."

In every advanced nation, women company owners play an important role, particularly in terms of their dedication to monetary developments. Recently, even among developing countries, women's participation in private enterprise has been increasing. The ground has been broken for women in business, and it seems that the growth has accelerated and is entering a new phase.

According to Kamal Singh, "A lady Entrepreneur can be described as a specific, imaginative and imaginative lady equipped for attaining self-monetary freedom exclusively or in a joint effort, produces work, and opens doors for others through starting, laying out, and showing the undertaking to staying up with her own, family, and public activity."

"Lady's business relies on ladies' collaboration in the value and effort of a commercial initiative," according to Ruhani J. Alice.

Ladies business Builders are thus those who conceive a business venture, launch it, assemble and combine the elements of creation, manage the initiative, accept risks, and manage financial vulnerability by owning a controlling stake in that particular activity.

A new approach that gives the female population greater importance has been accepted in our nation during this cutting-edge period of globalization and advancement. It has become essential for women to involve themselves in financial activities to continue helping their families as a result of the constant increase in the cost of the majority of common things.

They have shown their skills in various job settings and taken bold steps by approaching an unlawful location renowned for commercial ventures. Women have been conducting themselves as obvious businesspeople, dealing with obstacles, managing resources, admitting demands to achieve financial independence, and outlining key areas of strength for them in society.

Several facts on the status of women in commercial ventures:

In the USA and Canada, I. Ladies won 33% of private ventures.

ii. In Asian countries, women comprise 40% of the total labor force.

iv. When it comes to starting businesses, women in China outnumber males by at least two to one.
iv. Women have desires and strive to compete and succeed in all sectors on par with men.

Highlights of Ladies Business Endeavor

1. Most women with low wages will likely become entrepreneurs

2. Women who work in small workplaces will likely get into business for themselves.

3. The majority of female business leaders are married. They launched a business enterprise with their better half's support.

4. The majority of elderly women struggle to get financial support to start their projects.

5. A large proportion of women enter the professional world with almost little training or preparation.

6. Many women who require money get into business.

7. Maintainability and growth are due to the ladies' honesty and hard effort.

8. Women in business are more likely to be placed in security arrangements than in developments.

9. The majority of women prefer adjusting their salary and reducing their chances.

10. Female entrepreneurs' business ventures need working capital, which lowers net income

Why Do Women Enter the Corporate World?

1. Becoming financially independent

2. To plan their project

3. To present their personality to the public

4. To succeed in their endeavor with excellence

5. To create assurance for oneself

6. To encourage gambling with capacity

7. To ensure equal standing among the general population

8. To increase mobility and prominence of opportunity

Factors Affecting a Lady Entrepreneur

These factors suggest their requirement may be broadly categorized into two groups:

PERSUASIVE NEEDS

The compelling criteria that lead modern women to become business visionaries are discussed next:

1) Financial Need:

The movement of women is often another oddity in business. Due to the breakdown of the joint family structure and the need for additional compensation to meet demands for basic comforts despite growth or growing expenses, women have started to enter the most competitive sectors of business. As a result of this financial requirement, women have begun to join the business world to increase their family's income during the present periods of growth.

2) Desire for Great Achievement:

The strong desire for great success in one's life is another factor persuading women to join the corporate field. Despite what women are taught nowadays, they are unable to get jobs in the commercial center and are likely unwilling to leave their homes to work elsewhere due to family obligations.

As a result, a woman is unmistakably drawn by a desire to do something significant and demonstrate her abilities as a resource rather than as a member of the family. This is the most solid motivating factor for a woman to become a businessperson.

3) Liberty

The ability to live a free life with courage and confidence is another powerful idea that influences women to become businesswomen. A woman businessperson gains a high position, independent standing, and a sense of independence in public when she owns and controls a successful company.

4) Governmental Reassurance

Through autonomous efforts and endeavors, public authorities and non-governmental organizations stand out and promote women's financial conditions.

They have developed several plans for strategies and initiatives and introduced them to the nation's leading businesswomen who are women. These ideas for encouragement and motivation have led women to try business coaching.

5) Recommendation:

To qualify for autonomous employment in a variety of exchanges, occupations, livelihoods, and businesses of various kinds, women have been enrolling in various types of specialized, professional, modern, business, and specialist training. In areas where they may grow and flourish as persons on their own, offices are often offered to women. In the modern world, women have shown that they can perform on par with or even better than males in several categories of effectiveness, demanding labor, or knowledge.

6) Typical Job:

Like males, women feel jealous of those who use their might to promote the economy of their nation. In essence, our Indian women could aspire to act as important role models. They have actively entered a variety of professions, including politics, education, the social sector, organizations, and more. They are now making inroads into the corporate world, where they may demonstrate their importance just as they have in other disciplines.

7) Family Profession

A woman's desire to work in a privately held firm with her better half and other family members is strongly influenced by her family's employment. Women need to support their families financial activities, family businesses, and privately owned businesses to lower expenses and raise salaries for these businesses.

8) Workplace Age:

The ability of employers to provide opportunities is another driving force for women entering the corporate world. Women who work in business often take on jobs with a narrow scope, local businesses, or handicrafts, and they have a lot of potentials when it comes to starting their own company. In this way, they partly address the widespread problem of female unemployment.

9) Self-character and financial security:

Women desire to experience some economic security and public acclaim. Since they connect with unquestionably high-level authorities, clergymen, experts, and other people standing strong in high circumstances, women joining the commercial world may achieve such a position of self-personality and recognition of economic wellbeing.

10) Training in Mindfulness:

In addition to expanding in traditional bungalow businesses like toy production, bin making, and so forth because they require less specialized knowledge like the 3 Ps of pickles, powder (masala), and papad, women have been starting many other businesses that require more specialized knowledge like design, hardware, and many others as a result of the growth of education and female empowerment. Therefore, women in business are found in niche industries such as T.V. electronic ancillaries, small foundries, and capacitors.

To be able to provide their children with extravagantly expensive significant levels of clinical and specialized education and to lead an independent requirement of continuing in their life, women today would prefer not to stay inside the four walls of a house. Instead, they need to become, like their male partners, accomplishment-situated, vocation-disapproved, and financially free.

WORKING WITH NEEDS

it's a prerequisite for providing various offices for the success of women's initiatives. These are listed below:

1) Enough monetary offices

Regardless matter whether a corporation is run by men or women, finance is its lifeblood. Modern domains for women have been established by the public authorities.

Therefore, it should provide the anticipated financial offices to the female business visionaries to inspire them to launch their businesses or industries in such bequests.

Several financial programs, such as Mahila Udyam Nidhi, Promoting Improvement Asset, and others, have been established specifically for female business visionaries. Additionally, banks and development financing organizations can provide financial assistance to female company visionaries. When these positions are essentially free for them, women will be encouraged to enter the workforce.

2) Creative Thinking:

Women's imaginative thinking influences them to become entrepreneurs. Women with innovative skills and creative thinking are often encouraged to join a private firm or industry so they may convert their skills and abilities into a place of business endeavor rather than employment.

3) Family Support and Participation:

The complete cooperation and support of the family, particularly the husband, father by marriage, mother by marriage, adult children, tiny girls, and other people, if any, is another important factor that motivates women to start their businesses. Most women like having greater independence and financial opportunity in a modern, educated household. Therefore, they will often be eager to generate their kind of income from their company.

4) Accessibility of Skilled and Talented Women

Businesswomen of the future would be able to assign talented and experienced people to work with families. As a result, women will be motivated to pursue careers in business.

5) Projects for Improvement:

The Federal and State Legislatures have started a few new initiatives and are putting together programs specifically for women to help them become business visionaries. Such training and upgrading programs provide women with a variety of offices to start their businesses with freedom.

CHAPTER 2

Business Advice for Women With an Entrepreneurial Spirit

There are women with a visionary spirit of becoming an entrepreneur, therefore they must put some things in mind which are;

- Keep in Mind That It Demands Investment
- Join the forces with other Female Entrepreneurs
- Genuinely have faith in your abilities and your company.
- Be Your Organization's Essence
- Avoid delaying health insurance coverage.
- Get your picture in front of the crowd
- Be Persistent
- Your Own Tingle, Scratch

Keep in Mind That It Demands Investment

I have already managed many lash salons before starting The Lash Proficient. I made sure the salons were very efficient as well as solvable. I began my online company using the money I made from my most memorable venture. When developing your female-possessed company, keep in mind that it takes money to start making money. Don't let things go. Keep your regular job, assuming all else is equal, and create your business late at night.

Join Forces With Other Female Entrepreneurs

There are a lot of similar women starting groups, and there are many events focused on women. Some are headquartered regionally, in a certain sector, or even throughout the nation. Participate in these events to create a group with other female entrepreneurs with a vision. If you need a customer, a financial supporter, or someone to talk to about the problems of running a company, no one understands your predicament better than another female business visionary.

Genuinely have faith in your abilities and your company.

Your confidence should be the key tool in your arsenal while starting a company as a woman. On the off chance that you believe you can make it happen, you are almost there. A business initiative resembles a flight of steps and doesn't have a rigid structure.

It's important to maintain your confidence and understand that taking the difficult route ahead will benefit you since the world needs your devotion. As women, we can contribute to a creative business landscape that is unique, open-minded, and seeks to benefit the whole globe.

Be Your Organization's Essence

You should try to get as many people to see your online entertainment profiles as feasible if you're a business owner. To increase the perceived value of your independent business, you may make the most of your brand's significant areas of strength. By doing this, you will be able to gain the respect of people and increase their reliance on your company.

Avoid Delaying Health Insurance Coverage.

Although starting a business might be expensive, I urge my partners to think about doing so to invest money in a high-quality, comprehensive healthcare coverage plan. Although it would cost almost twice as much as it did when she worked for an employer that provided health insurance, a comprehensive plan that includes annual exams is important for women in particular. Given that it has historically favored men, it seems to sense that many new online publications don't address this. However, women should continue with annual exams and cancer screenings as if they were still enrolled in and insured by an employer-provided health insurance program.

Get your picture in front of the crowd

Find strategies for presenting yourself to the people who share your ideal interests. One way to draw attention to your things is by providing cost-free examples. Offer goods at local events that your desired interest group will attend. Create companies with well-defined powerhouses that are connected to your desired target audience and can provide credibility to your offerings. Your innovative journey will begin with using testing to spread the word about your company, setting you up for success.

Be Persistent

It may sometimes be difficult for women in business to join certain industries. Nevertheless, as any woman will attest, persistence is ingrained in our DNA. We may equip that resource to ensure that we don't accept "no" as an answer and that, if necessary, we'll go back to the planning stage. This desire propels us forward and creates a great model for the remainder of the business, where you'll see efficiency and innovation flourish.

Your Own Tingle, Scratch

For young entrepreneurs, the easiest way to start things going is to identify areas in your own life that you can improve rather than wasting time searching for problems that haven't been solved. With this mindset, it's far easier to find business ideas than it is to try to come up with outcomes for lengthy meetings to develop new ideas.

Anything that you're unhappy with, that doesn't exist, or that is carried out ineffectively, is an open door.

Women Entrepreneurs' Obstacles to Starting a Business and How to Overcome Them

1. Lack of Proper Support for Women in Business Visionaries

The lack of assets is one of the major challenges faced by female business visionaries. While many business visionaries find these challenging, female business visionaries are particularly adversely affected. Compared to male company leaders, women encounter more significant obstacles when trying to secure funding. This is even more true when it comes to investors and other financial institutions, who often justify their requests for funding and advances for their businesses.

This indicates that, in any case, the cycle that excessively favors their male partners nevertheless prevents female company visionaries from thinking of remarkable field-tested methods, spectacular credit records, and, shockingly, notable revenue. When they are fortunate enough to acquire the assets they need, they will have to deal with rising borrowing expenses. This eventually results in their organizations either collapsing or trying to survive over the long term.

Female entrepreneurs in Nigeria who have a vision for their businesses must approach reserves if they are to succeed. Because women who run successful businesses make a significant contribution to Nigerian culture, the government should make sure that she has access to all she needs to succeed in business. It's important to provide women business visionaries with some credit and reward opportunities. They should get advances in a manner that is comparable to that of their male partners.

2. Restricted Access to Hardware and Preparation

A person has to have enough knowledge about their field to succeed in business. In addition, they need sophisticated gear to carry out company operations. Entrepreneur must consistently demonstrate their abilities or run the risk of being supplanted by those in comparable professions who are more equipped.

Both male and female business visionaries may find it incredibly expensive to get basic tools and equipment. Some organizations have taken on the responsibility of making these preparations available to entrepreneurs at no cost or a subsidized fee. However, female business visionaries are in a challenging position, much like when gaining access to reserves. This is due to the preference given to male business visionaries who are assumed to be destined for success.

Sometimes women are portrayed as victims rather than clumsy idiots. Although the government is making progress by establishing several programs to help women, their efforts are often insufficient and inefficient in meeting the needs of female entrepreneurs.

3. <u>Cultural norms and practices</u>

The norms and traditions upheld by society constitute a further important challenge for female business visionaries in Nigeria. Men are often referred to be the heads of their houses in Nigerian social hierarchies. They are expected to take care of the house in that role, while women are seen as parental figures. They are expected to devote the bulk of their efforts to maintaining the house and being understanding toward their wives.

Imagine what would happen if a woman decided to deviate from the norm and get into business. She is seen by the public as trying to dominate her significant other rather than being receptive to him. As few men would support their women being anything other than designated housewives, this might create problems in their marriage.

In Nigeria, single female entrepreneurs are not exempt from these norms and traditions. The general society assumes that women should be content with becoming housewives; as a result, those who are single are often pressured into marriage. These women are also advised not to adopt professional practices that would prevent them from effectively defining their roles in the house. A business visionary gets discouraged by this tension. Female entrepreneurs need moral support to succeed in business.

Long-term, a few women have managed to break free from societal norms that prevent them from succeeding in a field that was formerly thought to be solely for men. However, a lot of women still have to deal with discrimination when they try to carve out careers for themselves as corporate leaders.

4. Concerns Regarding Female Business Visionaries' Capabilities

This particular test is an expansion of the division that female business visionaries saw as a consequence of most social order norms and conventions. There are allocated orientation-specific vocations and occupations in Nigeria, much as in other countries. This implies that certain professions are mostly reserved for males and that women are expected to adhere to particular professional or commercial practices.

Men are seen to be more logical for occupations that need a lot of physical strength and sharp thinking, for instance. In addition, a woman who engages in such is seen as inappropriate.

5. A lack of strong models and few mentoring projects

Female business visionaries should seek out top-notch mentoring if they want to have long-term success in any general population, especially in Nigeria. Most female business visionaries fall short of the level of moral support they need to prevent their enterprises from collapsing under the weight of adversity.

Female business visionaries would advance much by speaking with coaches, especially other female business visionaries who have experienced a similar situation. This may be quite challenging to locate since many female business visionaries are not yet at the top.

Women are not encouraged to take on difficulties, assess novel ideas, or represent broad organizations to society. Furthermore, there aren't as many female business visionaries as there are male-dominated ones, so there aren't as many role models to look up to or ask for advice.

You need to surround yourself with people who have successfully navigated the entrepreneurial journey if you want to succeed. When you are motivated in this way, you have something to look up to. Furthermore, you might tell yourself that if this person was able to make it happen, you can too. The question is if there is a limit to what a select group of strong female business visionaries can achieve. They are unable to fight everyone. because you may be trained by reading someone else's content without actually meeting them. At this stage, space is not a hindrance.

The world of company endeavors contains a lot of strain, which might very well discourage female business visionaries in Nigeria. Ladies must continue to thrive unquestionably as we keep pressing society to provide equal opportunities to both male and female business innovators. Break those glasses so we can keep winning.

6. A lack of flexibility

When women try to run a company in the open, they are looked down upon. All things considered, renting a space, buying a piece of property, or buying land is viewed with suspicion. The struggle is even worse for single women who run their businesses. Restricted adaptability also pertains to the showing of owning mechanical automobiles, and many financially independent women are unable to go alone due to safety concerns. This is only one of the many difficulties that the nation's female company leaders consider when trying to connect with potential customers.

7. Instruction is Missing

Having solid training in company management, organization, and money is necessary for maintaining an efficient business as a women business visionary in India. Customers expect female business visionaries to have core skills and around six years of education in a specialized sector. Tragically, the high costs of education in India have significantly hampered their ability to flourish. Only one woman in ten can afford to pay for expensive professional education or put in the time necessary to get them. To start up or change the educational scenario requires circumstance. However, this is altering, and many women are taking advantage of distance learning programs to remotely fulfill their qualifications.

8. Balancing Work and Family Life

Women are renowned for being the family's parents and children's mothers. When a woman runs a company, their schedules and requirements change. Moms must take some time away from their families to focus on business duties since it is unrealistic for them to run a company while being at home full-time. Families may argue as a result of not prioritizing family obligations, which makes many female business visionaries feel guilty. Business endeavor is not for the weak-willed, yet women approach it far more eagerly for this reason.

9. Serious rivalry

It is difficult to start ground-breaking ideas without any planning and scale them up in the modern economy. There is always someone out there who has the most current advances, thus female business visionaries need to showcase their skills to stand out. Due to the challenges and lengthy roads that lie ahead, neither associates nor financial supporters are eager to commit. Women must use their limited resources to work and grow their businesses. There is no believability in the most natural-sounding approach for them till they manufacture a solid reputation in the industry and enough advantages.

10. There are no backup plans

A select group of female entrepreneurs with vision who invest everything in their company is certain to fail. Female business visionaries are seen as lacking transparency and industry support since they lack education, financial security, work knowledge, and male assistance. They don't get serious treatment from peers, and those that invest everything into the company can't bear to fail or have a backup plan.

Today, computer literacy is crucial, and female entrepreneurs without a strong online presence will struggle to attract new customers. The majority of female business leaders need education in STEM fields including science, innovation, design, and math. They don't use the tools and processes needed to engage people and run a respectable company.

CHAPTER 3

The Executives Way a Woman Entrepreneur may Build others as a Side Project to her Business

There is no doubt that an individual's success in business may be significantly impacted by the assistance of several pioneers. When others in your company can identify with your struggles, they can help you move forward from a unique perspective and provide helpful advice when you need it most.

The assistance of other female business visionaries is an excellent way to boost that growth much further. For quite some time, women have been making enormous strides in the business world, reaching farther and higher than any time in recent memory.

1. **Invest in women-possessed organizations**

Entrepreneurs who identify as women should support businesses run by women. Indeed, we should mentor emerging female entrepreneurs and provide whatever advice we can because, at the end of the day, women need funding for their businesses and, regrettably, the bulk of that funding still goes to businesses founded by white males. If I ever sell my company, my goal is to use the proceeds to invest in as many businesses founded by women as I can since, in my opinion, doing so would significantly alter the makeup of who runs businesses. This includes both women of color and women of both sexes.

2. **Celebrate each other's triumphs**

Naturally, online entertainment and surveys should be available for celebrations, but interpersonal connections between people are important. Sending a word of congratulations to a single female business visionary is tremendously powerful. Recognize it when you see another entrepreneur doing something that fires your advantage or is deserving of praise. Individual references are also very important. When you come across something or a service that you like, spread the word!

3. **Help make women's voices heard.**

It could not be more difficult for women to continue working or to launch a company. Make a statement if you see an imbalance overall and support a cause that is relevant to women via online entertainment. Another important way to make a difference is to sustain yourself independently. For instance, encouraging female-founded businesses or mentoring younger women in business stimulates the local community of female business visionaries. Simply showing concern, mentoring your mentee, or introducing her to new opportunities will have a more significant impact than doing nothing.

4. **Deliver One Important Presentation**

While "supporting" or buying products manufactured by women may help in certain ways, it won't begin the significant transformation that a good presentation may bring about in a field. A long time ago, a male instructor of mine introduced me to his customer, a business owner. His customer, who is also my coach right now, sold her company for a few million dollars and has worked with me over the years to build up a strategy for a comparable outcome. One fantastic presentation is my most important tool for supporting other female business visionaries. Only one person has the power to alter their life. One of my Techstars mentees received her most notable financial support thanks to a simple introduction I made, which helped her amass pledges and build momentum toward a significant accomplishment. The impact of one presentation is that.

5. **Offer Your Thoughts**

As a female business pioneer, sharing your wisdom and exercising proactive compassion are the best ways to assist women in business. If any of your past mistakes or successes may help other women avoid making the same mistakes you did or offer them some great ideas, then you've achieved something positive without putting in a lot of effort. I believe that corporate leaders often put their interests ahead of those of their companies, maybe to gain an advantage. I acknowledge that being open and honest about your decisions might influence others. Engaging with organizations that support women in your sector and acting as a mentor or even an organization for other women in business is a great way to share your business expertise with other women.

6. **Create A References Registry**

Compiling a list of people working in a variety of businesses and professions is one way to help other female business visionaries. Ask her whether she would be willing to be on your reference list at the moment when you establish another association. When your company is expanding, a customer wants clear assistance, or a skill is needed that you don't possess, give other women the opportunity to collaborate or appreciate those referrals. People are often charitable, so if you can support another woman on her journey and help her reach her goals through important presentations, financially, or with helpful tidbits there is a strong likelihood that your desire to give and share will be reciprocated.

7. **Find out what they need.**

The most important thing that female business leaders can do to support other women in business is to find out what they need and then concentrate on providing it for them. Giving them the solution whether it's an asset, a presentation, or a methodology not only accelerates their success and generosity but also demonstrates the enormous knowledge of being an asset seller. It would create a revolutionary wave for women-owned businesses if every female business visionary frequently and purposefully provided other businesswomen with a few solutions each week and demanded that they demonstrate preemptive compassion.

8. **Promote Them Through Online Entertainment**

Sharing postings, disseminating information about products, and luring others in with them should make this achievable. People like to hear from other sincere people. These testimonials and real-life accounts promote the goods and services. Your followers will notice and get interested if you support a certain product and promote it. Now, that company may share your homage with their audience and see real people discussing the product. Businesses may store your comments and offers for online entertainment and use them in the future to advertise. Web-based entertainment is one of the most amazing methods to market for the great majority and it is a clear benefit for many people. Providing female support via online entertainment is easy and cost-free.

The Best Approach to Handling your Family and Business

1. **Understand Where to Focus Time and Energy.**
Owning a company and raising two young children suggests that one should be aware of where and what to prioritize. Event gurus and business visionaries alike may do more and do it better by focusing on the tasks at hand and refusing to let extraneous thoughts or distractions disturb the overall flow.

2. **Learn to think of yourself as accountable.**
Set goals, monitor them, and evaluate them. Take care of your presumptions. warmly congratulate you. Understand when you would truly want to rethink. Any business visionary who is committed to taking personal responsibility and being honest with themselves will be engaged in finding long-term success. Women should sincerely believe in themselves and their abilities.

3. **Never Feel Afraid to Ask for Help.**

When faced with a task that we don't have the foggiest notion how to do, there aren't enough hours in the day to complete, or we just can't make it happen, females business visionaries may discover their strengths rather than their weaknesses by learning how to ask for assistance. When we don't ask for assistance, especially in business, we waste time and resources that may be used to make a better effort.

4. **Don't wait even a split second to fall short.**

Women typically hold off on starting a company because they are afraid of being disappointed. Our reality would be much better if well-known and successful female business visionaries like CoCo Chanel, Ruth Controller (the creator of Barbie), Oprah Winfrey, Sarah Blakely (Spanx), and many others, let no one hold them down. Although fear is common, it may be overcome.

5. **Constantly Show Your Commitment.**

Being devoted allows female entrepreneurs to continue when their paths are not completely predetermined. It enables us to go on with our development and ascent to a higher level by removing the need for others' acceptance or approval.

6. **You want to have more faith in yourself than anybody else.**

Female business visionaries learn to be confident in themselves and stop looking for approval or recognition. Women entrepreneurs who believe in themselves may become sure and, as said before, concentrate on overcoming setbacks or challenges.

7. **Recognize your ideal interest circle.**

Business visionaries (people) routinely create businesses, products, and brands without ever defining their ideal target audience. Not only the buyer or customer is your ideal interest group; it also includes your representatives, colleagues, forces to be reckoned with, etc. All of these people might be resources in different ways.

8. **Continue to learn.**

There should never be a time when a female business visionary stops learning. No matter whether you're trying to master a skill or trade or learning a new one, continual learning creates a potential for growth, ground-breaking discoveries or ideas, and opportunity. The third remarkable technique to learn from others is to surround yourself with people who are successful in a field you are not. Finding a mentor, joining a driving force group, or enlisting a top management team to support your new enterprise are all important steps.

9. **Interact with Those Around You**

Female business visionaries may attract the most elite by not always demanding credit, by opening the door to others, including others, and so on. These elite individuals include the greatest representatives, coaches, customers, and so forth. Pay attention, be kind, be energizing, and engage in your company's innovative endeavors.

10. **Maintain Your Brand Image**

You may employ a brand's substantial areas of strength to boost your organization's permeability. Although Steve Jobs owned the Macintosh, Mac was marked by Steve Jobs thanks to the impact of his image. You may create pathways for people to turn their attention to you as the idea leader and, in turn, gain their confidence in your company by cultivating significant areas of strength for a brand.

11. **Encourage toughness, but keep your composure.**

The fact that women live in a world where people don't respect successful women is one of the toughest parts of being a great money manager in any field. Most of the time, driven and successful women are looked down on and their success is minimized. It is essential to sit down (or locate a suitable spot to sit) in any case, since there aren't many seats at the important tables for women in our society. Being tough is one of the most difficult but important things a woman in any vocation can learn; but, being responsive is also important.

12. **Gain From Mistakes**

Mistakes are a common feature of professional turn of events, and each successful businessperson has made their fair share of them along the road. The crucial lessons learned from mistakes help a business grow, endure, and advance.

13. **In any event, learn how to accept responsibility as well.**

Mistakes have a price to pay, no matter how big or little. In any case, accepting responsibility helps us stay grounded and focused on producing and improving. In the professional world, women should not be afraid to make mistakes; nevertheless, as mentioned in the suggestion that follows, by accepting responsibility, women permit themselves to feel in control.

14. **Learn how to refuse.**

Being able to say no is essential for female business visionaries. No to bad decisions, bad offers, time constraints, and even the difficult task of saying no out of concern that it would come off as impolite. Women are unable to achieve all of that and yet have a chance to grow and support their organizations. Learning how to say no enables us to learn how to deal with annoyance and how to learn how to put up with it without wanting to escape from it.

CHAPTER 4

Qualities a Woman Entrepreneur Should Possess:

1. Reliability

The foundation of a successful venture is trustworthiness, or keeping your word and upholding moral or ethical standards. Additionally, it fosters vital trust among people, from the team members you supervise to the partners and financiers you enlist to the customers you service.

People should adhere to a moral leader who is trustworthy because they should feel certain that they will be treated humanely and that their leader will put forth a heroic effort on behalf of the group. Additionally, to create an organizational culture that reflects such traits, moral behavior, dependability, and respect must start at the top.

2. Humility and an eagerness to learn

Sharp money managers understand that business cycles endure a long time. Because of how quickly business trends change, you might be cutting-edge today and outmoded tomorrow. Effective women in business continue to study and focus on rapidly adapting to the always-shifting landscape. When the open door appears, they become aware and humble themselves.

3. Adaptability and diligence

Whatever your orientation, business is challenging and full of vulnerability. The exam is made much more difficult by the larger responsibilities that women carry and the drop in professional vigor that usually follows having children. However, because of their adaptability and dedication, many women build companies. Nothing worthwhile in business comes easily. Sincere attempts and persistence in what you need are necessary for success. It takes persistence to become a skilled money manager.

4. Impulsive

Women are naturally stronger in some areas. Strong female pioneers may use their feel for direction in addition to using facts and knowledge to guide their decisions. In many situations, instinct is what steers them through both good and bad financial times.

Additionally, women are skilled at scanning their groups for prospective problems. By using this knowledge, they may create devoted representative groups that feel valued and understood.

5. Versatility

Making a move is essential, but it requires a thorough understanding of your customers, your sector, and your market. Pioneering women are curious and receptive to new ideas.

Being versatile properly enables us to anticipate changes for the company, which is crucial in this era of fast change fueled by innovation.

6. Relational skills

Authority and correspondence are still intertwined. Not only are women excellent speakers, but they are often also excellent listeners. Writing is more than just talking. Women naturally can read emotions and nonverbal communication. Ladies are fantastic inspirations for their groups because they have a deep understanding of what motivates others.

7. Compassion

Socialization has made women more empathetic. Normally, we serve as peacekeepers and protectors. The younger generations value spending time with their families and taking care of their mental health more than their elders did, and they want managers who understand their unique circumstances. By communicating on a personal level with their employees, managers may develop loyal staff.

8. A strong social support system

It is typical for successful women to support their female spouses, advocate for women at work, and aid others in moving up the corporate ladder. Women are more naturally drawn to assisting others and are less likely to be "solitary individuals" or "leaders of the pack."

As women, we should support one another and try to get support from others in our local communities, online, and in our businesses by affecting fundamental change and navigation.

Critical Areas to Focus on to Grow Your Business as a Woman Entrepreneur

1. **Keep a positive mindset**

Disregard all the metrics you may have learned about the failure and success rates of private enterprises in the first year or five. If you let other people's standards guide your life, you won't be able to run a successful company. So, aim to stand out by having a positive mindset.

Realizing that there will be obstacles but not fearing them is a key component of having a positive mindset. Regarding handling any problem that comes your way (many will assume you're a businessperson), dealing with everything with composure and sanity, and continuing in that loop. The widespread consensus is that women have stronger intellectual foundations than males do. You ought to use the same amount of energy to keep your company running. This is especially important since, because of the often biased and chauvinistic structure of social systems across the world, the problems faced by female business visionaries vary considerably from those faced by males.

2. **Soundly face the statistics.**

Numbers are reliable. You shouldn't be afraid of your income, perks, stock expenditures, or obligations (if any). It's okay if you don't make any money the first year, on the odd chance that you do. It's also okay if, on the odd chance, you don't make back your initial investment in the first year. This could have been the norm for even the best players when they first started, depending on the industry you're in and the product or service you're providing.

Find a trusted financial advisor and bookkeeper, then sit down with them to map out your company's financial structure and identify trends from prior years. Try to understand how things are related, such as how the benefit is affected, how much working capital is needed, the best stock measurement, etc.

3. **Understand and welcome displaying**

You could be providing the best product or service a customer could ask for. You and your employees may constantly put in long hours of labor. You may be chosen above every other candidate. However, until the target clientele is aware that your product or service exists, none of it matters.

Promoting involves some important steps, like educating potential customers about your product or service and establishing and maintaining long-term client relationships. However, before you can come up with a strong showcasing strategy, you must first determine the concept of your organization, your long-term objectives, and your target market.

As a woman, you can have an intuitive sense of understanding others, their sources of inspiration, and interacting with them in light of a shared goal. To promote your company, use your gut instinct and have trust in it.

4. **Value the people you represent.**

Each company has three key resources: money, property, and employees. Each is important, but if you ask any successful female business visionary, they will emphasize their people resources and representations. Private businesses that have a core of long-term, committed employees often grow far more quickly than those where the founder manages a one-lady operation with a continual stream of employees.

Respecting your politicians doesn't entail having open offices or party time Fridays. Consider your reps as real people with goals outside of their job descriptions. It suggests forgiving mistakes. You wish to discover and create your clan of employees as a woman starting a company. Women often have an advantage when it comes to understanding another person's perspective and building meaningful interactions. Use it to your maximum advantage.

In addition to hiring full-time reps, you may make wise use of specialists, seasonal employees, and assistants.

5. **Learn to trust others and delegate**

Your company is a child of yours, and you believe that you should handle every situation on your terms. In any event, it is never going to be how a firm can grow. The aforementioned action is crucial because it gives you the chance to enlist the help of important people who you know are capable of doing something just as well as you, if not worse.

You need to find out how to implement the board-by-exception concept. Just when everything seems to be going wrong, try to meditate. If not, you should concentrate on crucial tasks that will help you grow your company, form contacts, and expand your product or service.

CHAPTER 5

The Best Way For a Female Entrepreneur, to Adjust Business and Daily Life.

Business visionaries for women are not strangers to inspiration, deadlines, or goal-setting. Being prepared enough to complete tasks in business is a significant achievement. Finding a good balance between work and daily life may be a real challenge for the vast majority of female business visionaries. An enterprise requires challenging labor and many long stretches of information, which might raise expectations for day-to-day existence.

Finding a balance between work and family may be challenging for some female business leaders. We should look at how women entrepreneurs may juggle job and family obligations and maintain respectable daily lives while growing their businesses.

Time Management Is Critical For Female Company Visionaries

Time management is crucial in any business, but it is especially crucial for female business visionaries. You only have a certain amount of hours in the day before you truly want to focus on your loved ones, whether you telecommute or have your own office space. Making the most of such opportunities is essential for female business visionaries to advance. Start regularly planning and choosing the tasks that are necessary so that you may focus all of your efforts on them. Having designated energy for administrators, client calls, or emails might be helpful. Give routine tasks their time slot and adhere to them so they don't interfere with your personal life. Plan family time as well if you want to maintain a good balance between important and enjoyable activities. You'll be able to achieve a good balance and have the necessary downtime for you and your family if you set boundaries around your working hours so you have additional energy to devote to your family.

Innovation Can Be A Real Haven

For female business visionaries, innovation greatly simplifies life. The groundwork is in place right now for the majority of business innovators to telecommute at least sometimes. Financial experts that operate remotely may be flexible with their work schedules. When your kid is ill or the sitter is no longer available, you may block out time to go to an arrangement or stay at home without compromising your ability to work. The downside of innovation, of course, is that it has never been easier for work to intrude into your daily life. Being always available runs the risk of turning into business calls over dinner or not fully focusing on your children because you have one eye on your online entertainment accounts. For female business visionaries, innovation may be a haven but utilize it wisely so that it supports rather than disrupts your balance between serious and recreational activities.

Any entrepreneur with a vision understands that the correct group may have a big impact on their firm. Building solid foundations is essential to your success or lack thereof. The correct group may also significantly impact how well female business visionaries communicate across their work and personal lives. A trustworthy group of trusted representatives allows you to relinquish control for a day or an hour with the assurance that everything will still be running well when you return. A strong team means you may focus just on the important projects that need your involvement as an entrepreneur and designate more effectively. That translates to less time spent on tasks like administrator or customer help and more time to spend with your loved ones. Carefully evaluate the tasks you believe your group should do while selecting them. Build a team that complements your skills so that you may work more productively and be more flexible with family time.

Women in Business Encounter Explicit Challenges

Women in Business face explicit challenges that their male counterparts do not. For instance, your professional life must take that into account if you just had a kid and are still nursing or need to siphon milk. When it comes to making plans for child care, attending class, or emergency clinic visits, women usually shoulder a lot of the responsibility. Female entrepreneurs have an advantage since they may design their companies to meet their needs because they are in charge. For any busy parent, finding the appropriate balance between job and family life may be quite challenging. A good balance between important and enjoyable activities may be preserved and advanced by having a vision for the business. That suggests a more contented you and a happier everyday existence.

Methodologies for balancing daily life and work

Family and business are two of life's most important aspects. Trying to balance the two may sometimes be overwhelming since each requires a lot of thought and dedication from the person.

There will never be a guidebook on how to be effective guardians and make things work in ordinary life. As a company visionary, your only motivation is to explore new opportunities, develop working techniques, and achieve outcomes. You do this to advance financially, personally, and professionally.

However, when your family enters the picture, things might get a little confusing. Because you are today responsible for not just yourself but also your family, your work rate and outcomes need to increase. The attention you previously provided only to your company must now be divided and given to the growth of your new responsibilities, and balancing the two might prove to be a challenge.

The following advice will help you find that really important balance between the two, regardless of whether you're just starting your entrepreneurial adventure and considering starting a family in the future or are well-established down and dirty of the two.

1 **Establish a daily routine**

As full-time or temporary working guardians are aware, it is crucial to get to know the family. When a considerable amount of our time is wasted, it's common to feel both focused and worn out. Because of this, it is crucial that you, as working guardians, be conscious of how you allocate your energy. Create some structure in your day by following a daily routine that suits both you and your friends and family.

A standard not only keeps you organized and helpful but also makes your days less unpredictable and saves you money. Put aside a dispersed period for each project, both corporate and personal, and accept adaptation since things won't always go as planned.

Examples of flexible timetables you may start using right now include:

• Prepare a plan for the day each night for the next day.
• Schedule a time when you will check and respond to messages (for example once at 9 am and again at 6 pm).

2 **Complete your presence**

Working guardians often experience personal or professional setbacks. However, company visionaries typically experience a disorganized work process, excessive pressure, and shortcomings when interruptions seep in from other aspects of their lives. However, if you put too much emphasis on your family and neglect your company as a consequence, things might spiral out of control quickly. Being bamboozled hurts a lot, especially when we delay giving anything else our immediate attention. For this reason, it's crucial to show up for every job and to be entirely present at all times.

Imagine you had a little child who had just turned two around the time you were meant to join a load-up meeting. Where will you focus your thought?

Business visionaries must entirely focus on the primary task rather than juggling other responsibilities. Being fully present at your conference is not always a bad thing since, as a parent, you cannot and should not always accompany your children. Remember your true goals and the people you are doing this for to help you relax from the never-ending obligation you feel. Goodness, and it probably wouldn't hurt to research the finest toys for 2-year-olds on Top-Mother before leaving for that simple get-together so you know your youngster is well-cared for all around.

When your typical workday is over, you may return home and recommit yourself to raising your kid. The balance will eventually revolve around your company for a time. On your loved ones, and others. Don't ver-sweat the balance since it is delicate. Just be sure you stay on course in the here and now while taking that week's demands into account.

3 **Put Dinners First**

The most sacred moment in a family is during meals. You get to connect, catch up, and cultivate that culture of fellowship during these crucial windows of time. Families that share a meal are healthier and happier, according to research. Other benefits include a better manner of acting and competence, more reliability at home, and enhanced relationship traits. Additionally, as a parent, you're prepared to learn something new and beneficial about what your child or life partner accomplished that day, which will help you re-establish contact, strengthen bonds, and create stronger relationships.

Set up one night each day for family dinners to start, then progressively add more as you go. Additionally, make an effort to include the whole family in the cooking process. Not only will this help them learn more about nutrition and develop new skills, but it will also help them form enduring healthy eating habits since it is a fantastic way to interact with others.

4 Be Focused and Set Clear Goals

Though illustrating your company goals may be easy, have you tried to align them with your family goals? It is wise to have long-term goals and objectives for your company, but it is much more important to ensure the basic well-being of your family.

Have a clear (and realistic) goal for your family and company for each day that you spend there, and work toward achieving it. The goals will help you feel satisfied and recognize accomplishments as your family and business grow.

At some point, your family objective should include activities that you should do with them as well as things that you should do for them. Money goes everywhere, but your family's needs at home and their mental needs should be crucial for your day-to-day goals. So that you may spend it all together when you have free time.

5 **Hug maintaining one's health**

You'll most likely tend to see yourself as damaged. Giving your family you all demonstrate a crucial level of devotion, but this issue has not yet been resolved: who will deal with you? You could be the glue holding it all together, but stretching the glue too far weakens and fractures it. Neglecting your own mental or physical well-being might result in subpar performance as a parent and a leader.

Setting aside time to recharge and attend to your personal needs is crucial. You may revitalize and rejuvenate your mentality with stronger inventiveness, self-discipline, and thinking to face life head-on by turning off the main focuses in your life.

You can balance work and family successfully with discipline, an open mind, and confidence, and your job will support you.

CONCLUSION

There is no doubt that women must traverse a difficult path to show themselves in the field of entrepreneurship. Today's woman is courageous enough to stand out from the crowd, setting an example for others despite many obstacles in her path. She is exalted for her pre-feminist portrayal of women as domestic sacred cows. She balances her personal and professional lives, and it is up to us, the country's residents, to appreciate and admire her for that. Women entrepreneurs must first be encouraged to flourish if our nation is to be viewed as having a rapidly expanding economy on a global scale. A savvy woman can choose a career path, but by starting her own business, she can support additional women.

www.ingramcontent.com/pod-product-compliance
Lightning Source LLC
LaVergne TN
LVHW050337160826
845677LV00014B/3665

* 9 7 9 8 3 7 2 9 4 9 4 8 5 *